Lucie Stern
Palo Alto's Fairy Godmother

Lucie Stern
Palo Alto's Fairy Godmother

by
Michael Litfin

Palo Alto's Community Center, 1976

Palo Alto Historical Association
Palo Alto, California

Published by Palo Alto Historical Association
P. O. Box 193
Palo Alto, California 94302

The text for *Lucie Stern*, published by the Palo Alto Historical Association in 1998, is copyrighted © 1998 by Michael Litfin. All rights reserved including the right of reproduction in whole or in part in any form by the Palo Alto Historical Association.

This 2012 printing of *Lucie Stern* reproduces Michael Litfin's text, and it includes an Introduction, "Remembering Michael Litfin," copyright © 2012 Patricia Briggs; and an Addendum, "Peninsula Scouting and 'Aunt Lucie,'" by Larry Christenson, copyright © 2012 by Palo Alto Historical Association: editor-in-chief, Betty Gerard; image curator, Brian George; book designer, Harriette Shakes.

Photography credits: page *xi*, Patricia Briggs; pages 2–31, Palo Alto Historical Association Guy Miller Archives; page 38, Larry Christenson; pages 40–42, the Pacific Skyline Council, Boy Scouts of America and the Frank Livermore Scout Collection.

ISBN: 978-0-9638098-1-0
Printed by Omega Printing
Palo Alto, California

Palo Alto Historical Association
Palo Alto, California

Lucie Stern

PALO ALTO'S FAIRY GODMOTHER

Contents

❀

Introduction
Remembering Michael Litfin *xi*
Foreword *xv*
A Note from the Author *xvii*

Lucie Stern
The Early Years 3
Meeting and Courtship 4
The Wedding 5
A Word about Louis Stern 7
The Honeymoon 8
New York: Joy and Sorrow 8
Byde-A-Whyle 9
Daughter Ruth 14
The Palo Alto Years 16
The Community Center 22
Lucie's Other Gifts 29
Stanford's "Aunt Lucie" 30
Lucie and the Boy Scouts 33
Lucie's Death 34

Addendum
Peninsula Scouting and "Aunt Lucie" 39

❀

Introduction

Remembering Michael Litfin

Michael Litfin: a man who was talented, creative, capable, witty, supportive, imaginative, helpful, gifted, erudite, accomplished, responsible, kind, friendly, strong, gentle, honest, reliable, firm, fair, considerate, positive, humble, cheerful and so much more. This reissue of his 1998 book, *Lucie Stern: Palo Alto's Fairy Godmother*, is dedicated to the memory of his 32 years of devotion to the Palo Alto Children's Theatre located in the complex given the City by Lucie Stern.

Michael Litfin
1944–2008

Michael was born December 27, 1944, to Lela and Tom Litfin, the first of three boys, in the Land of 10,000 Lakes in Milaca, Minnesota. He went to Milaca High School where he enjoyed being in productions. His parents remember their pride when he received a standing ovation for his acting in "The Solid Gold Cadillac." He also played tuba in the school's marching band.

His interest in the theatre continued at St. Cloud State University, where he majored in Theatre, rejoiced in Theatre History and performing in plays. He was also a DJ and on-air interviewer for the college radio station. While in college he would go back to his high school to help in the drama department. His will specified that his extensive collection of books on theatre go to St. Cloud University.

Minneapolis is home to the prestigious Tyrone Guthrie Theatre and Michael was fortunate enough to study one summer with the great man himself. He also worked in summer stock, which proved useful when the Palo Alto Children's Theatre later began its own summer stock high-school and college company named Wingspread. After graduation and service in the Navy, he decided to enroll at the University of California Fresno to study for his Master of Arts in Theatre Management.

His contact with the Palo Alto Children's Theatre (PACT) began in 1975 when he brought a group of UC Fresno college students to perform at the Children's Theatre Conference held there. The theatre's young people were serving as hosts and hostesses, stage managers, house managers and technicians for the guest groups. Michael inquired about a position at the Children's Theatre and when one later became available, he applied. One of the many interview boards consisted of Alpha Crews, Candace Hathaway, Doyne Mraz and Joe Simitian. Though Michael had strong competition, he was hired in early 1976 as assistant director.

Michael's love of history was constant and the PACT was rich in history. He served two terms on the board of directors of the Palo Alto Historical Association. He enjoyed talking history with Birge Clark, Patty McEwen, George and Renton Crane, Wendell and Charlotte Cole and so many others. When he was asked to write a biography of Lucie Stern in 1997, he was delighted and sought out people who knew her, as well as source material from the media, museums and historical places relevant to her life.

He was the guest speaker at the Palo Alto Historical Association's public meeting January 1987 on "Children's Theatre: a Golden Anniversary." With his usual eloquence and sense of fun, Michael kept the audience both enlightened and entertained. A photographic retrospective of the Children's Theatre

Golden Anniversary was exhibited at the Civic Center and at five libraries. Michael and I were working on a history of PACT.

Michael enjoyed reading, writing, teaching, directing, designing, poetry, puppetry, needlepoint and travel, especially to Hawaii where he hoped to retire. He had a special gift for working with young people. In the words of one former Chldren's Theatre participant writing in the book of reminiscences published upon Michael's death from stomach cancer on February 1, 2008, "Thank you for giving of yourself so tirelessly for so many years, for giving your time, your energy, your passion, your craft, your spirit and mostly your deep humanity to provide a haven for so many of us growing up. You changed my life."

He changed the life of many other young people and more than 500 attended the celebration of his life. Michael was a marvelous colleague and faithful friend. He is greatly missed by me and by so many others whose lives he touched and enriched.

— Patricia Briggs
Director (retired)
Palo Alto Children's Theatre
July 2012

Foreword

Lucie Stern loved reading mystery novels. Yet she has become for most Palo Altans a mystery in her own right. For few still live who knew her before her "Palo Alto" years, and fewer still from those years knew her joys and sorrows. She was a private person, even while being a woman who reached out to others in ways that have shaped a Palo Alto century.

Fortunately, records provide clues to her nature and explain why and how she gained the love and appreciation of local generations she never knew and who never knew her.

— Michael Litfin

1998

A Note from the Author

I first became interested in Lucie Stern when I was hired at the Children's Theatre in 1976. It amazed me that a citizen had given the community such a wonderful gift. As the years went by, I gathered stories about her from former participants and staff members and members of the community. In 1987, when the Children's Theatre was celebrating its 50th anniversary and I was beginning to prepare the Children's Theatre archives, it became clear in discussions with the young people at the theater that few of them knew anything but the name Lucie Stern. It was fun to tell them stories about her and the theater. In 1992, I was honored to have been asked to serve on the Palo Alto Historical Association's Board of Directors. During one of the meetings on programming, someone suggested that I give a speech on Lucie since I always seemed to have stories about her. It became clear to me that much of the information I had gathered was myth or "hearsay." So I began an eight-month research project which had two goals: to provide a documented record of information about this great lady, and to provide the young people of today a picture of a real person who had joys and sorrows and who shared her blessings with her community.

My thanks to the Palo Alto Historical Association, particularly Barney Tanner, Ward Winslow, and Liz Hogan for their help and patience in transforming the spoken to the written word. Thanks to the many libraries and historical groups who shared information: Judah Magnus Museum, Berkeley; *Peninsula Times Tribune*; Mills College; President's Office, Stanford University; William Kramer, Ed., *Western States Jewish History;* Sally Bush, Atherton Heritage Association; Steve Staiger,

A NOTE FROM THE AUTHOR

Palo Alto Historical Association; Dr. Douglas Goldman, Strauss family genealogist; San Francisco Public Library; Sutro Library; California Historical Society, San Francisco; Alameda Free Library and the San Mateo Historical Museum. And to Patricia Briggs, Alison Williams, and Andy Hayes, Children's Theatre staff, who gave encouragement and assistance. Most of all, thanks to the young people of the theater who have asked questions about "Aunt Lucie" and who truly appreciate her gift to them.

— Michael Litfin
May 1998

Lucie Stern

Palo Alto's Fairy Godmother

Lucie Stern as a young woman

The Early Years

Published information about Lucie Stern before 1898 is sketchy—a few direct quotes appear in memoirs, but newspaper and magazine articles sometimes leave us with as many questions as answers.

She was born Lucie Cahen on April 16, 1871, in Sarrebourg, in French Lorraine, a town close to the Bavarian border. She was the third child of Louis and Henrietta Levy Cahen, whose oldest child was Sophie and whose second was Isadore. It is speculated that the family lived in France until Lucie was about three years old, when they returned to the United States. No information has been found that explains why the family had first come to the United States from France, then left the United States for a return to France, and then returned permanently to the United States. It is possible that Louis was in the importing business and may have explored the prospects for setting up business here on the first visit, or may even have established such a business on that first trip.

Upon their return to the United States, the Cahens took up residence in San Francisco at 1417 Franklin, in what Lucie is quoted as calling "a nice old-fashioned home." Today that location would be at the corner of Franklin and Sacramento streets on the Bay side of Van Ness Avenue, an area ravaged by fire following the 1906 earthquake.

The Cahens were at best estimation a middle-class family. Birge Clark, noted Palo Alto architect and friend of Lucie Stern, in his memoirs (available in the Palo Alto Historical Association archives) refers to Lucie's comment that her father was a "small cigar store owner." However, Langley's San Francisco Directory of 1883 (a list of businesses and residents) gives Louis Cahen's business as "Louis Cahen and Son, manufacturers of syrups, bitters, cordials, and agents for Bethesda Water, located at 418 Sacramento Street."

Lucie attended primary school on Turk Street. She is reported to have spoken often and fondly of her teachers and experiences there. Shortly before beginning high school, her family moved to Alameda, reportedly because of her mother's health. While living there she attended a French boarding school, probably because its curriculum included instruction in the family's native language. Sometime before she began high school the family moved back to San Francisco. After attending high school, she was sent to the Van Ness Seminary, where she is said to have learned "manners," a term that meant the social graces expected in late Victorian years. Her school acquaintances of that period are reported to have spoken of her as a "beautiful and charming girl."

She aspired to become a nurse—a choice she was forced to forego. As it turned out, however, nursing was required of her nearly all of her adult life, without the benefit of proper training. Instead of attending nursing school, Lucie stayed home to care for her aging and ailing parents. Her love for and duty to her parents, however, did not martyr her to a life isolated from society. Several newspapers mention her as a "prominent society belle."

Meeting and Courtship

It is likely that as a "society belle" Lucie had known her future husband before the Thanksgiving Day Party of 1898 at the Lilienthal home, a day Lucie later referred to as "the happiest day of my life." Whether or not that was the day Louis

Stern proposed to her or simply the day the two first met, we do know that their engagement was reported soon after in the December 2, 1898, edition of the weekly newspaper *Emmanuel.* The newspaper also noted that although no date had been set for the wedding it would be a short engagement.

The Wedding

A month after the engagement was announced, Lucie Cahen became Mrs. Louis Stern in a beautiful wedding held at the Palace Hotel in San Francisco on January 5, 1899. Lucie was 27 years of age, Louis 39. The fact that San Francisco newspapers all reported the event strongly suggests the importance of their wedding among San Franciscans. The following account (intentionally couched in the tenor of the news accounts of that day) draws on information that appeared variously in the *Examiner, Chronicle,* and *Bulletin.*

At approximately 4:30 p.m. on January 5, 1899, little Elise Stern, Louis' niece, led the bridal procession into the Maple Room of the Palace Hotel. She was dressed in white organdy trimmed with pink satin, with pink satin accessories. She carried the white satin pillow on which the ring rested.

Louis' nephew, Master Walter Heller, dressed in a black velvet suit, followed his cousin. Next in procession was Fannie Stern, another of Louis' nieces. She too was dressed in white organdy and pink satin and carried a bouquet of roses.

The maid of honor was Lucie's niece, Rosa Newmark. She was dressed in blue crepe with spangles and carried a bouquet of bridesmaid roses.

Escorted by her father, the petite 5'3" bride entered dressed in a gown of cream duchesse satin. Her skirt was cut with a short train and around the hem of the skirt was a ruching of tulle. The bodice of satin was low-necked and the tulle sleeves were "chirped to the neck," giving the effect of narrow shoulder straps. Her corsage was worn high and was trimmed with duchesse lace. She carried a bouquet of white orchids and lilies of the valley. Her sweeping veil was held with sprays of orange blossoms.

Waiting on the three-stepped platform at the end of the hall were the groom and Rabbi Jacob Voorsanger.

The traditional canopy supports on the platform were bound by ferns and white ribbons tied in "true lover's knots." Behind the rabbi on the altar was a large bouquet of white roses and golden candelabra. Behind the altar were rows of lighted candles placed among the greens.

The entire hall carried out the decor with wreaths of ferns and roses. John Housman was credited as the decorator of the rooms.

Following the ceremony a host of congratulations including more than 25 telegrams told them that friends in other parts were thinking of them. The reception lasted until 7 p.m. and included the ladies of the Cahen and Stern families assisting the young couple in receiving.

After being received, the 375 guests sat down to what was called a tête-a-tête supper, four to a table. The tables were decorated with autumn leaves that were carefully matched with the reds and yellows of the candelabra. There were toasts made and responded to.

One of the newspapers stated that "this was intended to be a quiet gathering... but indeed it turned out to be quite an elaborate affair."

A Word about Louis Stern

Lucie by her marriage to Louis Stern joined one of the foremost philanthropic families of the West Coast. It was her marriage that eventually provided her with the wealth by use of which she gained the sobriquet of "Palo Alto's Fairy Godmother."

Louis Stern was born February 12, 1859, in San Francisco. He was the youngest boy of six children, four boys and two girls, born to David and Fannie Stern. Fannie Stern was the only sister of Levi Strauss, whose given name is now a part of many world languages. David Stern is credited by William M. Kramer and Norton B. Stern in the article "Levi Strauss: The Man Behind the Myth," *Western States Jewish History*, April 1987, as having founded the firm that was to become Levi Strauss and Company. Exactly when or why David gave over the reins of the company to Levi is unclear; however, David Stern's four sons—Abraham, Jacob, Sigmund, and Louis—inherited the company upon the death of Levi Strauss in 1902.

By 1880, when Louis was 21, the Levi Strauss and Stern Company was listed as "importers of druggets, clothing, and furnishings goods." The word "importers" is significant because Louis is known to have attended to family business in France, where he would have known Denim, the town that gave its name to the famous cloth so common for overalls and such hardy clothing, and from which his firm obtained its supplies of material for the now world-famous pants.

In 1893, five years before Louis married Lucie, Levi Strauss was president of the firm, his nephew Jacob served as first vice president, Sigmund as second vice president, Louis as treasurer, and Abraham as secretary. Louis may have moved to

New York City sometime between 1894 and 1898 to conduct the importing and financial business of the firm (several news articles about the wedding mention that he resided in New York for several years).

The Honeymoon

Following their lavish wedding ceremony, the couple visited Southern California—presumably to see Lucie's sister Sophie Newmark—and then returned to San Francisco to gather whatever was needed before traveling to New York City and so on to Europe. Although their itinerary is not known, it is probable that they visited France and Germany on their traditional grand tour, possibly because of their family and business ties in those countries.

New York: Joy and Sorrow

On their return to the United States, the Sterns resided for several years in New York City. During these years Lucie suffered much of the heartache that she carried to her grave. She bore four children there, the first two of whom died in infancy. Louisa was born and died on June 18, 1900. Louis, Junior, born second, died October 8, 1901. In 1903, Dorothea was born and on April 25, 1906, Ruth was born a scant week after the San Francisco earthquake.

The great San Francisco earthquake of April 18, 1906, destroyed the Strauss-Stern residence at 621 Leavenworth Street, where the Stern nephews lived with their uncle, and the company building at 14 Battery Street. Fortunately, the company had opened an annex at 610 Clay Street in Oakland and was able to continue business despite the disaster.

This disaster seems to have figured in the return of Louis and his family to San Francisco from New York City. Exactly when Louis and Lucie returned to San Francisco with their two young daughters or where they lived immediately upon their return is not certain, but they may well have lived with either Abraham or Jacob, both of whom owned homes in Pacific Heights, which was not so seriously damaged by the earthquake. Louis had lived at the Leavenworth Street residence prior to his marriage to Lucie.

Quite soon after the earthquake, in the summer of 1906, Abraham, Sigmund, and Louis Stern bought more than 30 acres in Fair Oaks (later Atherton) just northwest of Menlo Park, the neighboring city north of Palo Alto. Louis built on his portion of this land almost immediately, for the *Emmanuel* (March 11, 1908) notes that having "sojourned the winter months at the St. Francis," the Louis Sterns were giving up their apartment soon "to reopen their magnificent home in Fair Oaks." The word "reopen" suggests that they may have lived in their new home a few months during the summer of 1907 before moving up to the St. Francis Hotel, for the 1908 season in the city.

Shortly after the Stern family returned to the Bay Area, Lucie's sorrows over her children continued with their loss of little Dorothea in 1908, at five years of age, from what was reported as pneumonia. By this time the Sterns were undoubtedly living at their new home, called Byde-A-Whyle.

Byde-A-Whyle

The two-story "home" called Byde-A-Whyle in Fair Oaks could better have been described by the reporter as a magnificent mansion. In 1907 Louis had the house designed in French Federal style by Currie and Currie of San Francisco and built on almost ten acres at a reported cost of nearly $30,000. The stately front gateposts and parts of the brick wall that surrounded the home still stand on Selby Lane in the Fair Oaks section of what is now Atherton.

Byde-A-Whyle, Fair Oaks home of Louis and Lucie Stern

The huge iron gates, which operated electrically, opened onto a lengthy curved drive to the house. Former Atherton Police Chief Leroy Hubbard recalled in an oral history (available in the archives of the Atherton Heritage Association) that when Louis drove home from work in San Francisco, he approached the massive gates, honked his horn, and Lucie pushed a button in the house to open the gates.

The house boasted an elevator, intricate inlaid floors, and a curved staircase. The family section of the home comprised seven bedrooms and four bathrooms. A servant area also was provided. The well-maintained lawns and three or four greenhouses and formal and country gardens required the care of four full-time gardeners. Louis and Lucie even managed, according to one story, to induce the chief gardener of the Prince of Wales to work for them. Another story tells that after Byde-A-Whyle was sold, one full-time maintenance worker was hired to ride a bicycle about the property just to turn sprinklers on and off.

So in Edwardian splendor Louis and Lucie hosted family, friends, and the famous. They gave dinner parties for Stanford notables and guests, as well as enjoyed visits from friends and relatives and trips to Palo Alto. During these years Louis Cahen, Lucie's nephew, attended Stanford University and may have contributed to giving Lucie a deep love for that university.

The Byde-A-Whyle years from 1908 to 1918 were surely active and joyful, yet the weight of human frailty and its consequences continued to darken lives of the Stern family.

One local woman recalls that as a child when visiting Byde-A-Whyle she was envious of Ruth, the Sterns' daughter, who seemed to her "like a fairy princess for she had a playhouse and secret garden and her own pony and cart." But any such envy would be short-lived. For Ruth changed at the age of 12 from what in his memoirs Birge Clark describes as a "normal, lovely and very bright young girl" to a young girl "stricken with epilepsy (grand mal) so that she now had to have a constant companion day and night, as a seizure would come at any time…" Another version of this turn of events has it that Ruth was all but ready for her coming-out party with grand preparations having been made, when this illness came upon her. This story may be partially true, although the event, because of her age, may well have been Ruth's Bat Mitzvah.

The year was 1918. What changed Ruth from the girl described by Clark could have been epileptic seizures which may have retarded her mental development and left her an invalid. The Clark memoirs indicate that Ruth had a nurse and three companions to care for her.

At about this same time, Louis was suffering serious health problems. Louis' nephew by marriage, Walter Haas, who joined Levi Strauss in 1919, stated that his uncle Louis was by then himself an invalid with what would prove to be a terminal illness.

So, from 1918 on, Lucie was forced to cope with two invalids at Byde-A-Whyle. During the years 1919 to 1924 the inhabitants of Byde-A-Whyle became secluded as Louis' disease progressed and Ruth's was beyond control. On June 30, 1924, Louis died at the age of 65 years.

Caring for Ruth remained Lucie's primary focus in life. The Clark memoirs tell that if Ruth had a seizure at a time when Lucie had guests, she would dismiss everyone to be with Ruth. Apparently Ruth was not allowed to leave the estate. When Ruth wanted to go somewhere, she was driven around the estate in a car, which would stop within the grounds for a picnic—a ruse that seemed to satisfy her that she had been away from home.

Lucie's last years at Byde-A-Whyle were less days of seclusion than of her dutiful presence as active caregiver to Ruth. But Lucie had many friends and visitors.

One of these, a Mrs. Crary, related that when she and her mother would visit and have lunch with Lucie, they often had

Lucie's favorite lunch, "boiled beef dinner with special horse-radish sauce." Chief Hubbard in his oral history told that when he visited Byde-A-Whyle, he was always offered and accepted a piece of cake and a big glass of milk. Eating was something Lucie enjoyed, and her concern for others sensibly included insisting that her guests should always eat plenty. A story has it that at one of her dinners Lucie tucked her napkin under her chin, turned to her dinner partner and said, "When you're rich, you can do this."

Lucie's fondness for good food showed physically, as one would expect. Years later in a tribute to the woman whom a Stanfordite had dubbed "Aunt Lucie," the *Stanford Observer* (June 1988) mentions Aunt Lucie's philosophy of food. It wrote, "Her figure was proof of her philosophy of food. It was built around a 5-foot-3 frame and indicated the effect of many full meals...the word that fits her best was *zaftig*...that fine old German-Yiddish word that means *juicy*—and, as applied to a woman, *buxom, plump, well-rounded*."

Almost to a person, those who knew her well enough to be invited to dinner or tea extolled the virtues of her French chef. But one need not wait for an invitation to a formal dinner to enjoy a meal with Lucie. You could, according to many accounts, simply be one of the people who might be helping repair something around the house, or who might have stopped only for a quick chat.

It was in such a situation that Palo Alto architect Birge Clark first met Lucie. He had stopped by Byde-A-Whyle to do some repair work on a porch, he tells us in his memoirs, when in true Lucie Stern tradition she invited him to lunch. He replied that he could not stop that day because he had to check on a $6,000 house he was building in Palo Alto. Lucie responded by saying, "My heavens, I had no idea you could build any house for $6,000. I think you had better build two, one for me and one for my daughter." And thus she and her favorite young architect began a lifelong friendship, and Lucie Stern began her move with Ruth to Palo Alto.

Daughter Ruth

For a time we must turn aside from our chief concern for Lucie's story and follow the thread of Ruth's life, for as the reader will soon see, Ruth's life was ever Lucie's deep concern thereafter.

Lucie's over-protection for Ruth became what we would today call an obsession. Her love and concern for her daughter seemed to broaden into concern for others, too. It was shown in years to come by the number of gifts given in Ruth's name to Stanford, the City of Palo Alto, the Boy Scouts of America, and other groups.

After Lucie moved with Ruth to Palo Alto from Fair Oaks in 1932, Ruth lived next door to her mother, in her own home at 1950 Cowper Street, until her death in 1972 when she was 65 years old. She survived Lucie by 26 years. These were quiet years. She was cared for with a lifelong commitment by the Charles D'Audney family, whom Lucie had selected sometime in the mid-1930s. Lucie had the house at 1928 Cowper constructed next to Ruth's residence to house the D'Audneys for as long as they lived. Mr. D'Audney was caretaker for the grounds, and Mrs. D'Audney, a trained nurse, served as Lucie's secretary and companion during Lucie's life, as well as helped her with Ruth, of course.

Ruth Stern at 3½ in 1909

Ruth was well provided for and cared for by the D'Audneys in the years following Lucie's death in 1946. She was under constant medication to control her epilepsy. She is said to have enjoyed visits to the Stern family home on the Monterey Peninsula. Ruth apparently was quiet and retiring. She enjoyed walking on the beach at Monterey and visiting some of the relatives of the D'Audneys.

Louis Stern's will had established a trust fund that Ruth could use with a conservator's approval until the age of 20. At 25, Ruth was to have access to one-half of the trust fund, and the trust was to be dissolved when she reached the age of 30. Before Ruth reached 30, however, her uncles, who were named as conservators, had died. It can reasonably be speculated from the wording of Lucie's will that Ruth's money from Louis was held in a trust to care for her every need throughout her life. Nonetheless, Lucie took the additional caution of designating part of her own wealth as a special reserve fund until Ruth's death in order to insure that her daughter would never be in need or lack care. And Walter Haas, Ruth's cousin, watched over Ruth's estate as executor, as well as Lucie's fortune after her death.

The Palo Alto Years

It was six years after Louis died that Lucie's Palo Alto years began in earnest. From the mid-1920s and perhaps earlier, Lucie had known many Palo Altans—Stanford professors, Palo Alto notables, and, of course, her own doctors, Russel Lee and Milton Saier. And in those years immediately following Louis' death in 1924 Lucie's focus on Ruth became truly obsessive. Doctors and friends sought ways to help Lucie find outside interests to relieve her stress.

To this end, Mrs. James Sharp, one of her closest friends, had brought Lucie to Palo Alto to see the Pendragon Players in the old Community House (now the MacArthur Park Restaurant), and also performances of the newly founded Children's Theatre. Mrs. Sharp is said to have urged her to move to Palo Alto. (Lucie's sister-in-law, Mrs. Sigmund Stern, a well-known San Francisco socialite and donor of the Sigmund Stern Grove, tried to encourage her to turn her attention back to participating again in San Francisco society. But Lucie said she would have none of it.) So Lucie may have been thinking about leaving her Fair Oaks mansion for Palo Alto even before meeting Birge Clark.

LUCIE STERN, PALO ALTO'S FAIRY GODMOTHER

In the early 1930s, Lucie and Ruth and retinue did move to Palo Alto. Lucie commissioned Clark to design and build adjacent homes for both her and Ruth at 1990 and 1950 Cowper Street. Mrs. Mary Edith Clifford remembered that while these houses were being built, Lucie lived for a time not far from the site in a small Spanish-style house.

Lucie's doctors were pleased to see how much joy she showed in building these homes and the gardens that connected them—one named the "Glorietta Garden" and the other the "Secret Garden." The latter name was prompted by the title of the popular turn-of-the-century novel by Frances Hodgson Burnett, which was a favorite of Lucie's, a novel she often read to Ruth. Byde-A-Whyle also had a "secret garden" area, and the name was later used for the secluded area for children built by Lucie for the Children's Theatre and Children's Library.

1990 Cowper Street, Lucie Stern's Palo Alto home

Building these homes gave Lucie additional pleasure because it helped the workmen and their families during the terrible years of the Great Depression. Her doctors were reported as seeing all of this as a means for relieving her moment-to-moment concerns about Ruth.

Birge Clark recorded a story that tells much about Lucie at that time. Shortly after she and Ruth moved into their new Palo Alto homes, Dr. Lee hoped that Lucie could be encouraged to enjoy going out more and not feel that she had to stay next door to Ruth so dutifully. So he persuaded Mrs. Sharp and Lucie to take an overnight trip to the Ahwahnee Hotel in Yosemite Valley, hoping that they would stay for several days.

The two women arrived at the Ahwahnee in Lucie's chauffeur-driven car and were placed in adjoining rooms with a communicating door. It must be noted that Lucie was the opposite of claustrophobic—that is, she always felt better when well-locked in. For example, she always locked her bedroom door at night and liked the fact that at Byde-A-Whyle an outside wall surrounded their house and that all house doors were always locked and checked. She had even discussed building a wall along the Cowper Street side of her new Palo Alto home—a wall that was never built.

Mrs. Sharp, on the other hand, was acutely claustrophobic. She could not stand being confined in spaces and always wanted her bedroom door unlocked so that if there were a fire or earthquake she could escape.

The first night in the Ahwahnee was a farcical disaster. After Mrs. Sharp thought Lucie was asleep, she crept into Lucie's room and unlocked the door to the corridor. Her own corridor door, of course, she had already left unlocked. But

Lucie was not sound asleep. She overheard. So when Mrs. Sharp had left, she arose, quietly locked her own corridor door and even went into Mrs. Sharp's room and locked her exterior door. Some time later, Mrs. Sharp awoke and decided to try her own door again. Finding it locked, she again entered Lucie's room only to discover Lucie's door also locked. So she unlocked them both again.

The poor women spent the remainder of the night locking and unlocking doors in turn, and in the morning decided to come straight home (perhaps exhausted)—which is what they did. Although Dr. Lee was much amused when he heard about the incident, the experience did nothing to reassure Lucie that she could leave Ruth and Palo Alto overnight.

Not long after Lucie moved to Palo Alto, she was seen attending, again at the request of her friend Mrs. Sharp, the productions of the Pendragon Players and the Children's Theatre at the old Community House. It so happened that a train on the nearby track from San Francisco seemed always to rumble past as if on cue in the middle of the first act of every play. It has become legend that Lucie thought this highly undesirable, if not downright upsetting. So the story goes that this annoyance is one of the reasons she had the Community Center developed with the new theater sited far from the railroad tracks.

Mrs. Louise M. Davies, major donor of San Francisco's Symphony Hall, and Birge Clark were reminiscing about Lucie one day when they were having lunch at the Children's Theatre. Mrs. Davies seemed quite certain that it had been all Dr. Lee's influence that the Community Center had been built. Certainly Dr. Lee and Dr. Saier did see how much fun Lucie had in building her homes, and they knew that she could afford to build and give something to the community. And, of course, it seemed helpful for Lucie's health for her to have something to focus on other than Ruth.

Whatever the mix of guiding motives and their relative strengths, Lucie Stern did turn her hand to becoming Palo Alto's benefactor. At a meeting of the City Council in 1932, Birge Clark formally addressed the Council with her offer by saying, "There is an anonymous donor who would like to give the city a community center, beginning with a donation of $40,000 to build a community theater." Previously this gift from an anonymous donor had also been announced following a meeting of the Garden Club, to which Lucie belonged. The offer, of course, did not stay anonymous for long. Soon the word was out that Lucie was the "fairy godmother."

Ruth and Lucie Stern with dog, Sally, in Ruth's home at 1950 Cowper Street.

It is of some interest that the wording presented to the Council included the comment that it was hoped the remainder of the center would be able to be completed fairly soon, depending on some degree to the access to funds. At that time, the comment about accessing funds is understandable. The nation was still in the throes of the Great Depression. Even the wealthy did not find it easy to "get at" their money. Birge Clark claimed that even the secretary of Levi Strauss and Company, who was handling Lucie's affairs, could never determine where she had found the money to build the theater.

It is possible that Lucie simply saved money from her personal allowance, which before probate had been $7,500 per month. It is also possible that Lucie expended some of Ruth's inheritance on the gift. According to Louis' will, Ruth was to receive her entire inheritance at age 30, but well before that age her wealth had been overseen by conservators, for the language of the will showed knowledge that Ruth was not able to handle her own affairs. Certainly Ruth never controlled her fortune during her lifetime. It is possible then that Lucie, by the early 1930s, had taken a major voice in if not sole control over the disposition of Ruth's inheritance. Lucie's brothers-in-law, who had been appointed by Louis' will as Ruth's conservators, had passed away. Some of Ruth's money may have been payable in some form that Lucie could have used. It is certain that the second part of the Community Center projet was named the Ruth Stern Wing and was identified as Ruth's personal gift.

But all this may be idle speculation considering the purposes to which all of the donated wealth was put. For the two things that mark the years of Lucie's life from 1932 until her death in 1946 were her maternal love and the generosity with which she showered gifts on her community, especially its children and Stanford University.

The Community Center

Palo Alto's Lucie Stern Community Center at 1305 Middlefield Road remains the magnificent gift that has given Palo Altans years of pleasure and enlightenment since 1933. It has been a place for them to learn from childhood to old age to appreciate the performing arts, and to participate in constructive and recreational uses of leisure time—all to the community's benefit. Today these buildings continue to offer programs that nourish Palo Alto's soul.

The Center is also the best-known work of celebrated Palo Alto architect Birge Clark, whose contributions to a Spanish Colonial Revival style both in public buildings and people's residences are noted for their innovative grace and his "signature" use of decorative tiles. The continued faithfulness to his style in additions to the center since his death has conserved the unity and beauty of his early conception.

The complex, such as it stands today, appeared in six stages. The first three parts were included in the original plan––the Community Theatre, the Ruth Stern Wing, and the Children's Theatre Wing. The last three—the Boy Scout Fire Circle, the Children's Library, and the walls and gates of the Secret Garden—were not envisioned in the original plan, but were additions by Lucie to the three initial wings. Each of these gifts meant growth and change in the personality of the community and the well-being of its citizens.

The Community Theatre––the first building in the complex, opened in 1933. It then accommodated both the adult and

The Community Theatre (c. 1933).

children's theater programs. How exciting it was for those in both groups to have a real stage on which to perform before an audience who could enjoy watching from professional theater seating.

The Ruth Stern Wing—The second facility of the center was the Ruth Stern Wing, a wing to meet the needs of all other activities previously carried out in the old Community House (presently the MacArthur Park Restaurant). This wing, built adjacent to and adjoining the west wing of the Community Theatre, was said to have cost $25,000. It was completed in 1935. The wing was comprised of a reception area, a main ballroom, and offices as well as a novel feature, an apartment at its north end, which housed the Center's caretaker-hostess. When the position fell vacant, Lucie requested that the Stanford Area Boy Scout Council should have use of that space. The City Council agreed.

The wing bears Lucie's daughter's name—an eloquent gesture expressing Lucie's love and devotion for her daughter and a telling sign that Ruth was never out of her thoughts. A plaque located at the main patio entrance to the wing states that the wing is a gift from Ruth Stern.

The Children's Theatre Wing—The third building was the Children's Theatre Wing, which sits parallel to and across the patio from the Ruth Stern Wing. These two wings plus the theater form a U around a brick-paved patio/courtyard.

For this wing Lucie specifically requested the City Council to designate its uses: the Children's Theatre and the Boy Scout House. The Children's Theatre opened on January 29,1937. The Childen's Theatre program had previously shared the Community Theatre, to the amusement and with the tolerance of the adults. Both programs had the goal of mounting a good show, but continued mutual use of just the one stage proved awkward and unworkable.

Undoubtedly, Hazel Glaister Robertson, founding director of the children's program, influenced Lucie's decision in this matter. Hazel was a charismatic and forceful leader and educator. She believed strongly that drama was the best tool for teaching democratic principles at an early age. Lucie designated the space for children's use only, so that adults would not usurp their province. The Children's Theatre therefore became a place, then as now, where young people could pursue theater arts skills on their own level of understanding, gaining social skills, and learning responsibility and teamwork, as well as an appreciation for theater as an art form.

Lucie asked the City Council to designate the north part of the Children's Theatre Wing as the Boy Scout House. Her two requests put the building under the administration of two groups: the Children's Theatre portion under the City Center Commission, and the Boy Scout House under the Stanford Area Council of the Boy Scouts of America. (This name has in recent years been changed to the Pacific Skyline Council.) The City Council endorsed and embraced her requests. At the time the Boy Scout area included a lobby, offices, restrooms, a general meeting area, and a series of troop rooms for various Palo Alto troops.

The Fire Circle—The fourth feature was given in 1938 and completed in 1939—the Boy Scout Fire Circle. Birge Clark related the story that in October of 1938, Lucie telephoned him and said, "I want to build something for the Boy Scouts." He admitted to her that both he and his brother and partner, David, were at a loss as to what more the Boy Scouts could possibly need. Finally, David came up with the idea of a ritual fire circle.

It stands today much as it did when constructed and has remained in use for Boy Scout ceremonies and other events. But it should be noted that the Boy Scouts have shared this space with others from the time it was completed. Early on the Children's Theatre produced summer shows there. Undoubtedly many will remember wonderful plays in more recent years produced there by both the Palo Alto Players and TheatreWorks.

The Children's Library—In 1939, Lucie decided to build a Children's Library at a cost of $17,000. At the time, Palo Alto had two libraries: a Carnegie Library situated downtown on the southwest corner of Hamilton and Bryant, where the Civic Center now stands, and a library in south Palo Alto (now the College Terrace branch). Although the City more or less ended at Rinconada Park to the east and California Avenue to the south, it was still spreading in those directions. There had already been talk about the need for another library in the south part of town.

The Community Center was the major center of community activity, much of which involved young people. Lucie therefore believed it fitting that the children should have not only their own theater, but their own library there—a place where their joy in books and stories could be expressed without their hearing the stern reprimand "Quiet!" This gift Lucie gave—took away—and then gave back, as told below.

In 1939–40 the City was struggling to accommodate a tight budget. Community services, of course, were looked to as the first place to make cuts. One councilperson thought Lucie's gift a good idea but believed the adult community should expect to use the new library as well; in addition, if the City accepted the gift, this person expected Lucie to endow the library for its future staffing costs.

When Lucie heard this plan, she let it be known that she was withdrawing her offer forthwith. Council members were shocked. They repudiated the one councilperson's suggestion and apologized to Lucie by letter, carefully averring that if the gift were forthcoming, it would be maintained and included in the City's budget under the Library Commission. The *San Francisco Examiner* said at the end of the announcement article in March 1940 that it had been agreed that "the City will bear the cost of maintenance and hire personnel for the library."

Thus the Children's Library, which was built behind the Children's Theatre, with its entrance on Harriet Street, became a dedicated reality, embraced by the Council on behalf of the people of the community.

The Secret Garden—The final area of the Community Center was to be the "Secret Garden," a name used today for the space between the Children's Theatre and the Children's Library. Before its development in 1940, it was described as a "mud hole in winter and a dust bowl in summer."

When Birge Clark was visiting the Children's Theatre one day, he was asked why Lucie had not built additions to the Children's Library and the Children's Theatre. Both facilities had been so popular that space, according to reports, was at a premium at both places. Birge replied, "She wouldn't give any more money to the Center. She thought she was done." And, he added, "it wasn't easy getting her to give the money for the walls and gates [of the garden]."

One can speculate that the earlier library fiasco may have caused Lucie to have doubts about the true appreciation of the community for what she was trying to do. Some have said that Lucie voiced her concern that people liked her only for her money, but one might suppose most wealthy public benefactors have been visited by that thought. Other Palo Altans have said that in negotiations it was always wise to agree with Lucie if one wanted to avoid experiencing her "queenly" attitude.

Robert Metcalf, former Children's Theatre staff member and Community Theatre worker in the 1930s, told a story about the planning meeting for the Secret Garden. He said that the initial idea Lucie had for the space was to plant an orchard. At that meeting, in addition to Lucie, were Mrs. Ralph Emerson Welles (wife of the Community Theatre director), Hazel Glaister Robertson (the Children's Theatre director), and Metcalf. Mrs. Welles, he said, dissuaded Lucie from her idea about an orchard. And thus the more practical idea of using the open space somehow for the two institutions that would border it was not lost.

The plan that evolved created a garden much like what we see today. Two quads were developed for the Children's Library: these were intended for outdoor reading and other activities. Two quads were also created for the Children's Theatre, one to serve as an amphitheater for summer shows and one for needed rehearsal space. The City was to provide landscaping for the project because at that time it had a municipal plant nursery.

Once the walls were up and the gates hung, Lucie wrote a letter to the Council asking why the landscaping had not begun. Between the lines, the letter can be interpreted as saying, "I've done my part. Now why haven't you started yours?" Lucie's prodding might also have been motivated by the library fiasco that had so recently occurred.

Publicly the *Palo Alto Times* urged quick action on the plan, for the hope then was to present the garden as a gift to the two facilities on the library's first birthday. But the plans that appeared in the *Times* were never realized. The hedges that were intended to reach ten feet in height never reached above seven or eight feet, if one excludes the arched entrances to quads. Pictures show that these hedges were kept at heights of only four to seven feet until perhaps the 1950s or early 1960s. Nonetheless the Secret Garden remained true to the initial vision, a place where children could work together on projects that interested them—a year-round space for building sets, for theater productions, and for classes, with the outdoor theater space kept open with grass seating for summer productions.

Lucie's Other Gifts

Though the Community Center was Lucie Stern's most magnificent gift to the citizens of Palo Alto, she was generous in meeting other needs not likely to be addressed expeditiously by the City.

For example, in 1940 she gave $15,000 to the Nurses' Cottage constructed on the southwest corner of the Palo Alto Hospital (now called the Hoover Pavilion). Lucie had recognized this need during a stay in the hospital. She discovered that nurses on what was called "broken service" had difficulty finding a place to rest and relax between shifts when time was too short for a quick visit home. This gift actually was made in Ruth's name, but was initiated by Lucie. The City agreed to clear the land and provide utility hookups. Perhaps Lucie's early interest in nursing prompted her kindness and thoughtfulness.

In 1945, Lucie gave the residence at 533 Forest Avenue to the Palo Alto Society for the Blind. At the dedication, Lucie made her last public appearance sitting in her car while her speech was delivered for her. Along with her remarks was a $1,000 check given "for some things they might need."

Lucie's final gift to the City while she was living was the Bird Sanctuary adjacent to and to the north of the "Duck Pond" (originally the old public pool) at the Palo Alto Yacht Harbor, which was completed at a cost of $9,700 after her death.

Gifts were also made to the City, Stanford University, and others from her estate and foundation after her death. These included:

- $2,500 to the Children's Theatre to fund a 1951 film that extols the virtues and the national and international reputation of the Palo Alto Children's Theatre experience.
- $25,000 in 1953 to help complete a $75,000 public contribution that would trigger a $225,000 City grant for the municipal golf course.
- $4,000 in 1954 to the Lawn Bowling Club for the construction of their clubhouse and $6,000 in 1973 for the expansion of the clubhouse.
- $33,000 in 1974 to the City to refurbish the patio at the Community Center.

The San Francisco Art Museum, Mills College, San Francisco State College, UC Medical Center, and a host of charitable, educational, and municipal bodies received gifts ranging from a few thousand dollars to hundreds of thousands of dollars from Lucie's estate/foundation.

For gifts to Stanford, see the following. For gifts to the Boy Scouts, see page 33.

Stanford's "Aunt Lucie"

The last time Lucie was allowed to go for a drive, she asked to be taken to Stanford. Stanford had honored Lucie several times. In December of 1941, she was made an Honorary Fellow and an honorary life member of the Associated Students of Stanford University. Both honors she cherished.

But one honor given to her by one of her "Stanford Boys" is remembered by everyone and meant more to her than all other possible honors. Phil Kennedy, Class of '33, gave her the title "Aunt Lucie." Lucie readily acknowledged this title, saying happily, "Now even Dr. Ray Lyman Wilbur (Stanford's president) calls me Aunt Lucie."

How appropriate the name, for it was as "Aunt Lucie" that she gave good home-cooked dinners to "her boys," helped them with financial needs, supported their dreams, and gave them a place in her home to express themselves and to meet in comfort with professors and other campus notables.

Frank Livermore, noted for establishing the American Heritage Museum of Palo Alto, was one of the young men who attended some of these dinners. He has said that most young men were invited because they were attending Stanford with

Lucie Stern, 1941, in a rare public photograph

scholarship help from Aunt Lucie or were, as he was, known to her from Boy Scouting.

It was Aunt Lucie who gave the community a place for leisure, work, and play, and for experiencing intellectual growth. It was Aunt Lucie who brought ice cream cones to children after a hard day of rehearsing, and who on Halloween could be counted on to give out those big 10-cent candy bars. It was Aunt Lucie who always had smooth sidewalks in front of her house that promised a wonderful place to roller skate, and it was as "Aunt Lucie" that she signed cards and letters to friends.

It was Aunt Lucie who had a closet the Stanford boys appreciated, for it contained pants and shirts and sweaters. Each fellow was invited when leaving to pick out a little gift for himself. Now almost everyone who mentions Lucie's "closet" does so in remembrance of her Stanford boys. But she had gifts for ladies too. Several ladies whose mothers visited Lucie received little wrapped gifts of lotions or other appropriate sundries. The occasional girlfriend who would be invited to accompany her Stanford boyfriend to visit was not forgotten either. Each was said to have received a pair of silk stockings.

Another legendary and maternal story is that Aunt Lucie kept a running correspondence with many of her boys. One article said at least three dozen of them held regular correspondence with her. Her hospitality was not limited to her Stanford boys or professors. Should parents of "her boys" be in town, she was always said to have "been at home" for them.

During her lifetime she gave Stanford and its students an estimated $900,000 through her student loan fund and gifts to the health services. After her death, her estate gave $600,000 to build Stern Hall, a rather interesting dormitory building with a 1940s look. The estate also gave $3,000,000 to the Law School's new building, making her estate the largest donor up to that time. In addition, the estate gave the funds to build the Faculty Club. Gifts also have included an endowed chair (The Lucie Stern Professorship in Social Sciences), the Research Laboratory, the Children's Free Bed Fund for the old Convalescent Hospital, and a playhouse at the Children's Hospital. All totaled, Stanford reported in an article that Lucie and her estate and foundation had contributed $6.5 million to the University.

Lucie and the Boy Scouts

Next to her Stanford Boys, Lucie held the Boy Scouts closest to her heart. Some of the gifts she gave them have already been mentioned (see pages 24–25). In addition she gave them the camp at Huntington Lake in the High Sierra and a station wagon to get there. She gave money to furnish its building and supply a good cook stove. She gave them $20,000 for a foundation. She built the Sea Scout base at the Palo Alto Yacht Harbor for $12,000. Most of all she gave them attention and moral support.

In 1939 when she was 69 years old, she hosted a tea for the mothers at the Community Center and asked her friend Palo Alto author Kathleen Norris to speak. Kathleen's reply was, "Dear Lucie, of course I'll be with you on February 1, at the Boy Scout House, Community Center. At about four, I suppose. We have to stand back of our boys, and it's in line with your usual magnificence that you've helped carry them over their lean year. Affectionate good wishes for 1939 and always. [Signed] Kathleen."

The Scouts in turn loved their Aunt Lucie. In 1945, they honored her by presenting to the Community Center a portrait that shows her seated in her Stanford room looking through one of her Stanford scrapbooks. Four or five accounts of the portrait's unveiling remark on the effusive gasp heard when the painting was unveiled.

Birge Clark, in his memoirs, and several other attendees at the event who were interviewed spoke of their great shock and disappointment in the painting. Birge commented that he was "outraged" when the painting was unveiled. It seemed to him to present Lucie as a typical club woman, with an air of superiority far removed from her kind and motherly expression.

This life-size portrait by Renaud Hoffman was the first likeness Lucie had allowed to be made of her throughout the many years she had been benefactor and fairy godmother to the community. The portrait was done in five brief sittings. The presentation was made by the President of the Stanford Area Boy Scout Council, George Harding. Mrs. Paul Merner, City Council member, accepted the portrait for the City in the absence of Mayor Byron Blois and acknowledgement of the gift was by Dr. Dorsey Lyon, Chair of the Community Center Commission. The portrait now hangs in the hall of the Ruth Stern Wing.

Lucie's Death

For almost two years, 1944–45, Lucie was not well. In fact, she became a semi-invalid. She had heart trouble and suffered from hypertension. On January 18, 1946, after lapsing unconscious two days earlier, she quietly passed away in her home. Shortly before she slipped into unconsciousness, she asked her companion and secretary, Mrs. D'Audney, to read her the chapter on beauty from her book compiled by Dr. Harry Reynolds and his wife as a gift for their friends.

Her funeral was held at her home. Her coffin had an honor guard of Boy Scouts, and her pallbearers were all Boy Scouts and Knights of Dunamis. The Reverend George Whisler, who had headed the Boy Scout program and the Community Center Commission during Lucie's close connections with both groups, read from the Bible Lucie had given her daughter and also from her own Bible. From Ruth's he read, "I will lift mine eyes unto the hills…" and from Lucie's "and now abideth faith, hope and love, but the greatest of these is love…"

It was love which guided Aunt Lucie, love which allowed her not to dwell on the many tragedies of her life but to seek ways for giving to others, and in so doing, find her own happiness. Her credo was "The things that make others happy are the things worthwhile."

Addendum

The Boy Scout Fire Circle, completed in 1939, was restored in 2002 by the parents, Scouts and friends of Troop 57 (photo: 2012).

Peninsula Scouting and "Aunt Lucie"

For more than 75 years, hundreds of thousands of Scouts, Scout leaders and community friends have enjoyed the unique Scout facilities of the Palo Alto Scout Service Center and Camp Oljato. In an open letter to the Scouts in 1944, Lucie wrote in part:

> Realizing that we in America must be awake to our responsibility in preparing our young men for citizenship, and believing that the Boy Scout Movement has proved its worth in this respect, I felt that, in providing for the activities to be housed at the Community in Palo Alto, provision also should be included for scouting activities. For that reason, the present Scout Hall, Troop Rooms, Patrol Rooms, and the Ruth Stern Fire Circle were constructed and set aside for the exclusive use of Boy Scout Activities.

After Lucie and Ruth Stern moved from Atherton to Palo Alto in the early 1930s, Lucie made a series of gifts to the City of Palo Alto for a community theater complex. Her initial anonymous gift of $40,000 for the theater in 1933 was followed by $25,000 in 1935 for the Ruth Stern Wing, which included an apartment for the caretaker-hostess. In 1938 was added the Children's Theatre Wing, with the north part designated by the City Council as the Boy Scout Hall at Lucie's request. A final addition, the Fire Circle, was completed the following year.

Originally part of the Santa Clara Valley Council, the cities of Los Altos, Mountain View, Stanford and Palo Alto petitioned the National Scout Office to form a new Council in northern Santa Clara County. In January 26, 1940, the inaugural dinner was held in the Community Center's Ballroom. In 1940, Lucie requested that the newly formed Stanford Area Council be given use of the Apartment, fondly referred to as the "Lucie Stern Apartment," as their new Council Headquarters Office. The City Council agreed. Over the years, the space has been used by the Scouts for meeting, training and storage.

As the Stanford Area Council formed, a search for a High Sierra summer camp continued. In 1940, a location was found on Huntington Lake at the 7,000-foot elevation. In 1941, Scout leaders were able to raise a $1,000 deposit, needing a remaining $5,000 option to purchase campsite rights from the U.S. Forest Department. Several weeks later a $5,000 check from Lucie Stern was received at Council headquarters. In 1941, use of the pristine Camp Oljato was secured in perpetuity.

Tom Wyman was a young Scout attending the 1941 summer Camp Oljato Camp Fire the night the camp staff made the historic announcement. He wrote:

> It was during the summer of 1941 that Boy Scouts of the Stanford Area Council first attended what became Camp Oljato on Huntington Lake in the High Sierras. The setting of the camp was wonderful amid 14 acres of tall trees by a sheltered cove on the lake's cold blue

Scouts swimming and rowing at Camp Oljato on Huntington Lake (c. 1941).

waters. That first year there was no telephone or electricity, and the camp was accessible only by boat from Lakeshore. We enjoyed several day-long outings into the adjacent "wilderness" areas and built a rickety bridge across a rushing stream near camp to earn our Pioneering merit badges. As a young Scout at the time, one of my clearest memories was our campfire circle on by the lake under starry skies when we first learned that Aunt Lucie Stern had made it possible with her personal gift of $5,000 for the Stanford Area Council to acquire our camp. We shouted ourselves hoarse that evening to make certain Aunt Lucie heard us all the way down in Palo Alto and that she knew how much we appreciated her generosity. In addition, we each wrote a letter of thanks to Mrs. Stern. Those of us who had attended summer Scout camp on Lake Oneonta the year before knew that this was a special moment for Palo Alto and Stanford Area scouting. We didn't appreciate just how *very special* it was.

Since that wonderful first summer at Camp Oljato many years ago, the camp has become a cherished memory for thousands of young Scouts and their counselors who, over the years, have enjoyed summer camp on Huntington Lake. Aunt Lucie's legacy lives on!

Camp Oljato was dedicated in 1942. "Oljato" has a Navajo Indian origin and means "Starlight on the Water." The dedicatory plaque and camp emblem consist of "the landmark Jeffrey Pine and the two Stars over the water signifying the ideals of Truth and Knowledge. These Stars also symbolize the Donors of the Camp and several of its buildings… Aunt Lucie Stern and Ruth Stern."

On May 30, 1941, Lucie Stern, who had given $13,000 for a Sea Scout Headquarters, christened the building by smashing a bottle of Atlantic Ocean seawater on the deck rail. In 1985, when the Palo Alto Yacht Harbor was closed, the Sea Scout operations were moved to Redwood City. The Palo Alto Sea Scouts began in 1928 and has been in continuous operation. In 2012, Sea Scouts celebrate their national centennial birthday. The old headquarters building, recently restored, will soon open as the EcoCenter in the Palo Alto Baylands Nature Preserve.

The Boy Scouts' "Aunt Lucie" (c. 1942)

Lucie passed away January 18, 1946, after two years of failing health.

As a living tribute to Lucie's generosity, Scouting continues to "prove its worth." In the summer of 2002, the Stern Fire Circle was restored. In 2004, the Palo Alto Scout Hall was restored. A new Camp Oljato Handicraft Lodge was funded and built in 2007, replacing the first of many aging camp structures. In 2009, the Apartment was restored and now includes a chronology of newspaper clippings and photographs of the Stanford Area Council era.*

Our community has been blessed with the remarkable generosity of Lucie Stern. As Michael Litfin noted, her credo was "The things that make others happy are the things worthwhile."

— Larry R. Christenson
Board Member
Pacific Skyline Council,
Boy Scouts of America
Eagle Scout (1961)
July 2012

Note: The Stanford Area Council and the San Mateo Council merged in 1994 to form the present-day Pacific Skyline Council.

The Palo Alto Historical Association

Palo Alto Historical Association (PAHA) is a non-profit organization that works to collect, preserve and make available to the public information about the history of Palo Alto through programs and newsletters, publications and digital resources.

The association maintains the Palo Alto Guy Miller Archives, a collection of films, videos, oral histories, photos, records, letters and ephemera. More than 12,000 historic photos are digitized with over 3,000 posted on PAHA's website. The archives are open to the public. All images reproduced in *Lucie Stern: Palo Alto's Fairy Godmother,* unless specifically noted, are from these archives.

PAHA invites readers' interest and participation. To find out more about the association's activities and programs, review the list of publications, pursue an interest in local history scholarship, or become a member, visit *www.pahistory.org.*